SQL

Learn SQL in 24 Hours Or Less

A Beginner's Guide To Learning SQL Programming Now

Table Of Contents

Introduction 4
Chapter 1: Fundamental Concepts Regarding SQL and Databases 6
   Relational Databases 7
   The SQL Language 8
   The SQL Statements 9
   The Different Execution Types 10
Chapter 2: The Environment of the SQL Language 12
   SQL's Environment – The Basics 12
   More Details About SQL Catalogs 14
   The Schemas 14
   How to Name Database Objects 18
   How to Generate a Schema 20
   Creating a New Database 22
Chapter 3: How to Generate and Modify Tables 24
   Generating an SQL Table 24
   Specifying the Data Type of a Column 29
   How to Specify the Default Value of a Column 35
   How to Alter an SQL Table 36
   How to Delete an SQL Table 39
Chapter 4: How to Ensure Data Integrity 40
   Integrity Constraints – The Basics 40
   The Not Null Constraint 41
   The Unique Constraint 43
   The PRIMARY KEY Constraint 46
   The FOREIGN KEY Constraints 50
   The CHECK Constraint 60
Chapter 5: How to Create an SQL View 68
   How to Add a View to a Database 68
   How to Create an Updateable View 76
   How to Drop a View 77
Chapter 6: Database Security 78
   The Security Model of SQL 78
   Creating and Deleting a Role 80

Granting and Revoking a Privilege 81
Conclusion 83

Introduction

In this book you will find practical tips and detailed instructions on how to learn the SQL language in just one day.

This eBook will teach you the most important aspects of SQL. It will give you theoretical explanations, realistic examples, actual syntax and lots of codes. If you're looking for a comprehensive guide about the SQL language, this is the material you're looking for.

By reading this book, you'll learn about a wide range of SQL-related topics. Here are some examples:

- The different types of databases
- How to use SQL for a relational database
- The different types of SQL commands
- How to create a database
- How to give/revoke account privileges to users
- How to create tables and columns
- How to customize columns
- The different data types in SQL
- How to apply constraints on tables and columns
- How to work with related tables

- How to enter new information into a database

You can certainly benefit from this eBook even if you have never programmed anything before. This eBook will teach you the basics of SQL programming and give you the syntax of important SQL commands. If you want to become a skilled SQL programmer in just 24 hours, get this eBook now and read it carefully.

Let's begin the journey

Chapter 1: Fundamental Concepts Regarding SQL and Databases

This chapter will teach you the basics of the SQL language and the relational databases. By reading this material, you'll know how the language works and how to use a relational database.

The Databases

SQL (i.e. Structured Query Language) allows you to create and maintain relational databases. It also allows the management of information inside those databases. Before discussing SQL further, let's define what the term "database" means. People use this term when referring to a collection of information (e.g. names, phone numbers, addresses, etc.) that is organized according to a definite structure.

Here are the most common structures used in modern databases:

- Hierarchical – This structure uses parent-child relationships. It organizes information through nodes, which are the counterpart of tables in relational databases. Parent nodes can have multiple child nodes. Child nodes, however, can have just one "parent." The hierarchical structure is extremely popular, although it is inflexible and doesn't support complicated relationships.

- Network – The network structure solves the problems found in the hierarchical structure. Here, you will organize information into "record types." This structure arranges information into a system that links pairs of records: members and owners. A record type can work with other record types. Thus, a network database supports complicated searches and relationships. The main disadvantage of this structure is its complexity: you need to know how the structure works and how information is stored.

- Relational – This is the most popular structure these days. A relational database addresses the issues linked with network and hierarchical databases. In a network or hierarchical system, you'll rely on a particular database implementation, which you will "hard code" onto the database application you are using. You need to adjust the database application whenever you add items to your database. In a relational database, however, you won't have to worry about your application. You may alter your database without affecting the application itself.

Relational Databases

Since you will use SQL with relational databases, we need to discuss this kind of structure in detail. The main element of a relational database is the "relation", which are essentially groups of rows and columns placed in a table that represents one object. An object (also known as "entity"), on the other hand, consists of related information.

Entities are things, events, places, persons, or concepts about which information is gathered. Each relation consists of different columns (which represent attributes). Attributes are units that define or characterize entities. For instance, in the table given below, the entity is a book with size, color, and weight as attributes.

Name_of_Pen:Brand	Pen_Size: Size	Pen_Color: Color	Product_Weight: Weight
Pen A	Small	Red	Light
Pen B	Medium	Yellow	Heavy
Pen C	Large	Blue	Heavy

In this table, all of the attributes have a domain (i.e. the name that specifies which type of information you can store in the attribute). You shouldn't confuse attributes with data types. Data types are particular kinds of constraints (i.e. tools used to secure information integrity) linked with columns, while domains describe what information you can include in the attributes associated with them. For instance, the attribute named Product_Weight is linked with the Weight domain.

Important Note: It would be best if you will use a domain that describes the attribute it will hold. Although this approach is optional, it can help you improve the usability and readability of your database entries.

The SQL Language

SQL is a computer language designed for relational databases. However, this language isn't a database implementation. Although the relational structure gives the core elements of a relational database, SQL supports the actual implementation of this kind of database.

SQL, one of the most popular languages today, is not similar to other programming languages (e.g. Java, C, C++, etc.). Most programming languages are procedural, which means they define how a program must perform its functions. SQL, which is a non-procedural language, focuses on the results of a program's functions. The software environment you're using will determine the database application that will complete its tasks.

The SQL language lacks the programming features of other languages. This is the reason why some programmers refer to SQL as a "sublanguage." Basically, you will use SQL with other languages (e.g. C#) to perform tasks.

The SQL Statements

SQL has different types of statements that you can use in managing a database. In this section, let's divide SQL statements according to their functions:

- DDL (i.e. Data Definition Language) – These statements allow you to generate, delete, or modify database objects (e.g. schemas, triggers, tables, etc.). The most popular statements of this category are CREATE, DROP, and ALTER. For instance, you must use "CREATE TABLE" to generate a new table, "ALTER TABLE" to change the properties of a table, and "DROP TABLE" to remove the information regarding a table from your database.
- DCL (i.e. Data Control Language) – With these statements, you can specify the people or programs that can access the objects inside your database. Using DCL, you may give or take away access using "GRANT" or "REVOKE," respectively. You can also use DCL statements to manage the kind of access database users have to your information. For instance, you may set which database users can edit a

certain block of data.

- DML (i.e. Data Manipulation Language) – A DML statement allows you to add, modify, delete, or retrieve information stored inside your database entries. The main keywords of the DML category are: UPDATE, SELECT, DELETE, and INSERT. You may use "SELECT" to retrieve information from a database table and "INSERT" to add information.

The Different Execution Types

The SQL language has different binding styles (or execution methods). These methods don't just influence the execution of the statements: they also determine which SQL statement will work with any given binding style. Here are the four execution methods that you'll encounter while using SQL:

- Direct Invocation – This method allows you to communicate with a database using a front-end program (e.g. Management Studio, iSQL*Plus, etc.). You may enter your database queries into the program and run the SQL statement. Your computer will return the search results after some time (the timeframe involved depends on your machine's computing power). SQL users consider this as an excellent way to view information, check relationships, and verify database entries.
- Module Binding – With this method, you can generate sets of SQL commands that are separate from your main programming language. Once you have created a command set, you may incorporate it into a database program using a linker. Command sets (also known as "modules") hold "procedures," which contain the SQL commands you're working with.

- Embedded SQL – With this binding style, you will encode (embed) SQL statements in the main programming language. For instance, you may encode an SQL statement inside the source code of a C# program. Before compiling the code, a preprocessor will analyze the SQL commands and separate them from the C# statements. Then, the preprocessor will convert the SQL commands into a format that the database management system can read. The C# code will work as normal.

- CLI (i.e. Call-Level Interface) – You can use this binding style to execute SQL statements using an interface. Here, you will pass SQL commands as arguments to one or more subroutines. The system won't precompile SQL statements as it does in module binding and embedded SQL. Rather, the database management system will run the said statements directly.

Important Note: The examples you'll find later in this book will use direct invocation. That's because this binding style is compatible with ad hoc database queries and produces results immediately.

Chapter 2: The Environment of the SQL Language

This chapter will focus on the SQL environment. It will explain language catalogs and teach you how to create databases and schemas. Read this material carefully: it will help you learn the SQL language in just one day.

SQL's Environment – The Basics

The environment of this computer language is the totality of the elements that form that environment. All of these elements work together to perform SQL functionalities such as querying and storing information. When combined, these elements create a base structure for database management systems.

SQL's environment consists of six different elements. The SQL server/s and SQL client/s belong to the implementation of the language: database users consider them as mere subtypes.

Let's discuss these elements in detail:

- SQL Agent - This is the structure that executes SQL statements. This element can only work within the limits of the SQL client used in the implementation.

- Authorization Identifier – This element represents roles or users that can access the data and objects inside the environment. "Users" refer to the security accounts that represent applications, people, or system services. "Roles," on the other hand, are sets of predetermined access privileges that you may assign to users or other roles.

- SQL Implementation – This is the element that runs SQL commands according to the SQL agent's needs. An "implementation" involves a client and a server. Here, the client will connect to the server and keep information that is relevant to the interactions between the former and the latter. Meanwhile, the server will manage the session that occurs during the connection and run SQL commands sent by the client.

- Client Module – A module is a set of SQL commands that you wrote separately from another programming language. It holds varying numbers of externally triggered processes, with each process consisting of one SQL command. The client module of SQL exists inside the environment and runs through the language's implementation.

- Routine Mapping – This element links SQL-triggered routines with foreign server descriptors.

- User Mapping – With this element, you can pair authorization identifiers with foreign server descriptors.

- Site – A site is a collection of tables that hold SQL information as defined by the schemas' contents. SQL users refer to the information within a site as "a database."

- Catalog – This element is a set of schemas grouped together within a particular namespace. Catalogs hold the data schema, which involves the descriptors of different schema objects.

Important Note: Schemas are containers for data objects (e.g. domains, tables, views, etc.). You'll learn about this topic in the next section.

More Details About SQL Catalogs

As stated earlier, the environment of SQL is the combination of all the elements that form that environment. Well, SQL catalogs involve the same logic. SQL catalogs are groups of schemas; if you'll combine these schemas, you will be able to define namespaces inside the environment of SQL.

Important Note: Namespaces are naming structures that indicate related elements in a given SQL environment. Database users often depict a namespace as an upside down tree. This image represents the hierarchical (i.e. parent-child) relationships of data objects.

You may also think of SQL catalogs as hierarchical structures with the catalogs as the top-level (i.e. parent) objects and schemas as the sub-level (i.e. child) objects.

The Schemas

You'll find schemas in each SQL catalog. Schemas are groups of related data objects that belong to the same namespace. Schemas serve as containers for these objects. Keep in mind that each object stores SQL information or conduct information-related processes. The schemas, the objects they contain, as well as the data inside those objects, belong to the authorization identifier linked with those schemas.

The Information Schema

All SQL catalogs contain "INFORMATION_SCHEMA," which is one of the most special schemas in this computer language. The "INFORMATION_SCHEMA" holds information regarding different schema objects (which are "views" most of the time). Views are virtual tables that allow you to see information gathered from real database tables. Using a view, you may show the data about objects within that SQL catalog as if it is SQL-based information.

Schema Objects

You'll find schema objects at the lowest portion of the SQL catalog structure. A schema object is a group of related elements that exist inside a schema. This level of functionality is the one involved in data storage. Thus, you need to be familiar with it if you want to be a successful SQL programmer. You can use the SQL language to define an object, change that definition, and save and/or alter information inside that object. Actually, almost all of the things you will be reading from here on has a connection with schema objects.

Here are the schema objects that you'll encounter while using SQL:

- View – You can invoke this schema object to create virtual tables. The tables won't really exist – the database will just run and store the SQL command that describes those tables. After invoking the command, the view will pull information from a base table and show the results of your query as if you're looking at an actual base table.
- Base Table – This is the basic data unit in SQL. A base table consists of rows and columns and is similar to the

relational theory's "relation" (i.e. with its tuples and attributes). The columns are linked with data types and contain related values. For instance, a base table for books will have columns that hold information about those books (e.g. titles, authors, genres, etc.).

- Domain – You may specify this object while defining columns. Domains rely on the data type specified by the user, but may hold constraints and default values. Constraints help you in limiting the information that a column can store.

- UDT (User-Defined Type) – SQL allows you to specify a UDT while creating a column. The SQL language offers two kinds of user-defined types: structured and distinct. A structured type consists of different attribute values. A distinct type, on the other hand, is completely based on a data type of SQL and its values.

- Constraint – This is a limitation that you need to place on a domain, table, or column to restrict the kind of information that you can add to the database object you're working on. For instance, you may use a constraint to make sure that a particular column can only hold numbers within a certain range.

- Server Module – This schema object holds SQL-triggered routines. Basically, a module can contain routines, procedures, or SQL commands. An SQL-triggered routine is a process or function that you can invoke from the SQL language. Keep in mind that processes and functions are kinds of SQL commands that may accept parameters (i.e. the values you'll give to a command while invoking it). Functions may receive parameters and return values depending on the information included in their statement. Processes (also known as "procedures") may take values and give out parameters.

- Trigger – This is an object linked with a table. It specifies the action/s that the system must perform when something happens to the table it is associated with. The database actions that can activate the "trigger" are table updates, deletions, and data insertions. For instance, if you'll delete a row from one table, you might activate a trigger that deletes information stored in a different table.

- SQL-Triggered Routine – This is a process or function that you can call from SQL. In general, this kind of routine can take the form of a stand-alone schema object or a module-dependent object.

- Character Set – This set of attributes specifies how the database must represent characters. Character sets have three different attributes, namely: form-of-use, default collation, and repertoire. The "form-of-use" attribute specifies how characters will appear as data strings to software and/or hardware. "Default collation" specifies how the database will compare strings. Finally, the "repertoire" attribute specifies the characters that the system can express.

- Collation – This the collection of rules that determine how a database must compare strings that are inside a single repertoire. You can use this information to arrange the characters. In SQL, you need to define default rules for all of your character sets.

- Transliteration – Basically, transliterations are SQL operations that map the contents of a character set to the contents of a different set. Transliterations may involve other SQL operations such as character translations (i.e. from lowercase to uppercase).

- Sequence Generator – This is a mechanism that you can use to generate consecutive integers. A sequence generator stores the current value - that value will be used in generating other sequences of values.

How to Name Database Objects

The previous sections focused on theoretical and supporting information. This approach of explaining the SQL language aims to help you master the basics of SQL. This way, you will be able to understand SQL statements once you're in that part of the book. At this point, there's just one more fundamental topic that you need to study – the object identifiers. Identifiers are names that you'll assign to SQL objects. In this computer language, an object's name can have up to 128 characters. In addition, each name should follow the predetermined conventions. You may assign an identifier to any database object (e.g. views, tables, schemas, etc.) that you will generate with SQL commands.

A common identifier is restrictive and needs to follow the rules given below:

- It is not case-sensitive. That means Book_Title is identical to BOOK_TITLE.

- It can contain underscores, letters and numbers. For instance, you may create First_Book and 1st_Book as the name of your views. As you can see, you need to use an underscore to separate words. You can't use spaces or dashes while naming SQL objects. Actually, this language treats a dash as the "subtraction operator" (you will learn about the operators later).

- It cannot contain any reserved keyword of the language.

Important Note: Keywords are words that have special functions in a computer language. In SQL, keywords may belong to one of these categories: reserved and non-reserved. As its name suggests, you can't use a reserved keyword aside from the function it is intended to be used for in an SQL command. A non-reserved keyword, on the other hand, doesn't have any restriction.

This language is "case insensitive" when it comes to common identifiers. Actually, it will change identifiers to uppercase while storing them. This is the reason why SQL considers First_Book and FIRST_BOOK as identical names.

A "delimited identifier" is not as strict as a common identifier. However, it should still follow certain rules. These rules are:

- The name should be inside a pair of double quotes (e.g. "First_Book").

- The database won't store any quotation mark. However, it will store the identifiers as you wrote them in your SQL commands.

- It is case-sensitive. That means "First_Book" and "FIRST_BOOK" are two different names. However, "FIRST_BOOK" and First_Book are identical (since SQL converts all regular identifiers to uppercase).

- You may use any character.

- You can use any word, even the reserved keywords of SQL.

Qualified Identifiers

SQL qualifies the identifier of each schema object based on its position in the environment's hierarchical structure. A qualified identifier contains the name of the object, schema and catalog involved (i.e. you need to separate these values using periods). For instance, let's assume that you're working on a table called Book_Authors. This table is located in a schema named Book_List, which is stored in the Book catalog. The qualified identifier for this table is Book.Book_List.Book_Authors.

How to Generate a Schema

At this point, you've become familiar with the naming conventions of the SQL language. It's time to write SQL statements. Let's start with "CREATE SCHEMA" since schemas are top-level objects in the SQL structure. While learning a new computer language, you should always begin with the syntax of the statements being discussed. Here is the syntax of CREATE SCHEMA:

CREATE SCHEMA {identifier clause}

[{the path or character set}]

[{the elements of the schema}]

Important Note: The curly braces hold data that represents a clause or value associated with that data. For instance, {identifier clause} represents the values and keywords you used in naming the new schema. The brackets, however, signify the optional clauses of the syntax. SQL doesn't require you to set paths, schema elements, or character sets while creating a schema.

Let's analyze this syntax in detail. Here, "CREATE SCHEMA" are keywords that inform SQL regarding the task you want to complete. These keywords come before {identifier clause}, which is a placeholder that contains the schema's name. In SQL, you may add an authorization identifier to your CREATE SCHEMA statements. You can do this just by adding AUTHORIZATION (i.e. another SQL keyword) to the identifier clause of your command. Thus, the identifier clause may take any of these forms:

- {schema identifier}

- AUTHORIZATION {name of the authorization}

- {schema identifier} AUTHORIZATION {name of the authorization}

The {name of the authorization} part specifies the owner of the schema. If you won't specify any value, the system will assume that the owner is the current database user. If you didn't include a schema identifier, the system will use the name of your authorization to generate the missing information.

The next part, {the path or character set}, lets you assign default paths, character sets, or both. You should type DEFAULT CHARACTER SET before the character set that you want to use. The path, on the other hand, sets a search pattern for SQL-triggered routines (i.e. functions and procedures) that are generated through the CREATE SCHEMA command.

The final clause of the syntax consists of different kinds of SQL commands that you may add in the current statement. In most cases, you can use this clause to generate various schema objects (e.g. domains, triggers, tables, etc.). The main benefit of this feature is that you can add objects to your schema during the creation process.

Now, let's discuss an example of this kind of statement. The code given below generates a new schema called "LIBRARY." Also, it will set USER as the authorization identifier and Latin2 as the character set.

CREATE SCHEMA LIBRARY AUTHORIZATION USER

DEFAULT CHARACTER SET Latin2

CREATE TABLE FICTION

(AUTHOR_ID INTEGER, AUTHOR_NAME CHARACTER (25))
;

As you can see, this example creates a table called "FICTION." This is an element that you can specify inside the last clause of the syntax. Keep in mind that there are no limits regarding the statements that you can add. The statement given above generates a table that has two columns: AUTHOR_ID and AUTHOR_NAME.

Creating a New Database

The SQL language doesn't have a command for creating a database. However, you will likely use an RDBMS (i.e. relational database management system) that supports the generation of database objects and the utilization of those objects in managing information. For this reason, if you want to take advantage of the projects and samples included in this eBook, you need to generate a sample database. With this approach, you may manipulate information without losing important data from a real database.

Most database products support commands that create database objects. For instance, MySQL, SQL Server, and Oracle have "CREATE DATABASE" in their built-in SQL languages. However, the parameters you can define, the permissions you need in executing the command, and how systems implement a database object differ from one database product to another. Fortunately, almost all database products utilize the same syntax to generate database objects:

CREATE DATABASE {name of the database}

{extra parameters}

Before generating any database, you need to read the documentation of the product you're using. Additionally, talk to the database administrators to make sure that you can add databases to your SQL environment. After creating a database, you may generate schemas, views, tables, and other kinds of objects in that database. Then, you may start populating the tables with the appropriate information.

Chapter 3: How to Generate and Modify Tables

In SQL, tables serve as the primary tool for managing data. Almost all of the programming you'll do is linked to one or more tables. Consequently, prior to inserting data into a database, you need to make sure that the correct tables exist.

This chapter will teach you how to generate and modify an SQL table. Read this chapter carefully – it will help you learn SQL in just 24 hours.

Generating an SQL Table

This computer language supports three kinds of tables: (1) base tables, (2) derived tables, and (3) viewed tables. According to SQL users, a base table is usually a schema object that contains SQL information. A derived table, on the other hand, is the result that you'll see when querying information from a database. Lastly, a viewed table is a different name for a "view," with the definition saved inside the schema.

This section will focus on base tables. Actually, almost all of the samples and projects you'll see in this eBook involve base tables. However, base tables have different characteristics. Some tables are permanent (also called persistent) while others are temporary. There are module-based tables and there are data objects. All module-based tables are temporary. Here are the base tables that you'll encounter while using SQL:

- Persistent Base Table – You can define this schema object using the CREATE TABLE command. A persistent base table contains the SQL information you stored in a database. This kind of base table is extremely popular. Actually, people often refer to a persistent base table whenever they talk about "tables" or "base tables." This table will exist while its definition exists. In addition, you can call it from any session.

- Declared Local Temporary Table – You will declare this table as a process inside a module. The definition of the table isn't stored within the schema. Also, it won't exist until the procedure runs. Just like any temporary table, you can only use a declared temporary table during the session you've created it in.

- Created Local Temporary Table – To create this table, you need to use the CREATE LOCAL TEMPORARY TABLE command. You can only use this kind of table during the session it was created in. Additionally, you need to be inside the correct module in order to access this table.

- Global Temporary Table – You must use the command CREATE GLOBAL TEMPORARY TABLE to generate this schema object. Even though its definition belongs to the schema, the table will only exist if referenced inside the session it was created in. That means the table will disappear as soon as the related session ends. This temporary table is called "global" because it allows you to use its contents at any part of the current session.

Important Note: In SQL programming, "sessions" refer to the connections between SQL agents and database users. During a session, the user will invoke a set of consecutive commands. On the other hand, a module is a database object that holds routines, processes, or SQL commands. You'll learn more about modules in later chapters.

Keep in mind that you can use "CREATE TABLE" to generate any kind of base table except a local temporary one. The remaining part of this chapter will focus on permanent base tables. Here is the syntax of the CREATE TABLE command:

CREATE { [LOCAL | GLOBAL] TEMPORARY } TABLE <name of the table>

< (element of the table) { [, (element of the table)] . . . } >

{ ON COMMIT [DELETE | PRESERVE] ROWS }

Important Note: You should read the pipe symbol (i.e. "|") as "or." Thus, you must choose one of the two options given for each appropriate clause.

For the syntax given above, the curly braces group data elements together. The initial line of that format groups the LOCAL | GLOBAL keywords together. Here, you must decide how you will manage the contents of the braces and know how they can function in the clause. For the first part of the syntax, you need to choose either LOCAL or GLOBAL with TEMPORARY, but this is optional.

The three dots you see in the next line show that you may repeat that part as many times as you need. That means you can add any number of "(element of the table)" clauses to your command.

In the first part of the current syntax, you may indicate whether you want a temporary table or a permanent one. You can also set the table's name. Thus, you may use one these variants:

- CREATE TABLE (the table's name)
- CREATE GLOBAL TEMPORARY TABLE (the table's name)

- CREATE LOCAL TEMPORARY TABLE (the table's name)

The next part of the format lets you determine the elements that form the table (you'll learn about that later). The final line, however, applies to temporary tables only. You can use this line to set whether the new table will delete all of its contents once the COMMIT command runs. You can use the COMMIT command to implement modifications to your database.

You may consider the (element of the table) clause/s as the main part of the CREATE TABLE command. This part allows you to define the elements (e.g. constraints, columns, etc.) of the table you want to create. In SQL, you may define any number of "(element of the table)" clauses. If you will define multiple clauses, you need to separate the entries using commas.

Let's analyze the syntax for defining a new column:

(the column's name) [(domain) | (type of data)]

{ (the default clause) } { (the column's constraint) } { COLLATE (the collation identifier) }

The syntax's initial line requires you to set the column's name and choose a domain or data type. You'll learn how to specify the data types of your columns later in this chapter. The next line, however, allows you set a collation, a default value, or column constraints.

Here's a basic example of the CREATE TABLE command:

CREATE TABLE AUTHORS

(AUTHOR_ID INTEGER,

AUTHOR_NAME CHARACTER (50));

This command creates a table called AUTHORS and two columns. The name of the first column is AUTHOR_ID while that of the second one is AUTHOR_NAME. The former is linked with the INTEGER type of data. The latter, on the other hand, belongs to the CHARACTER type. As you can see, you need to use a comma to separate column definitions.

You probably noticed that the column definitions are located in different lines and that they are aligned because of extra spaces. This style of writing SQL statements help you in improving the readability of your codes. The SQL language doesn't require these spaces of newline characters. However, you should use this style as much as possible.

If you will run the command given above, you will see a table that looks like this:

AUTHOR_ID: INTEGER	AUTHOR_NAME: CHARACTER(50)
1001	Stephen King
1002	Arthur Conan Doyle
1003	E. L. James
1004	Charles Dickens

Important Note: You won't see any data entry inside the new table. The information shown in this example are included to help you understand what kind of table the current command creates.

At this point, let's discuss how you can specify the data type of your columns. You need to master this topic since data types play an important role in the creation of any column.

Specifying the Data Type of a Column

When defining a column, you should always set its name and associated domain or data type. The domain and data type limit the information that the column can accept. For instance, certain data types restrict the values of a column to numerals. In SQL, a data type belongs to one of these categories:

- Predefined – These data types are extremely popular. Basically, a predefined data type is an element that restricts values based on the criteria set for the database. This category consists of five data types, namely: string, interval, numeric, Boolean and datetime.
- Constructed – A constructed data type can contain multiple values. Thus, the data types you'll find in this category are more complex and powerful than traditional ones.
- User-Defined – A user-defined data type is based on a predefined attribute definition or data type. You need to add it to your SQL environment as a schema object. In SQL, a user-defined data type can either be structured or distinct. A structured data type uses an attribute definition as its template. A distinct type, on the other hand, requires

a predefined type as a template.

Let's discuss each data type in detail:

The Strings

A string data type allows you to set values according to data bits or character sets. The values you use may be fixed or varying in length, depending on the data type you are currently using. In SQL, the string data type has four subtypes:

- Character String – With this subtype, you must choose the allowed values from a certain character set. You may use a default set or one that you have defined while creating the column.

- National Character String – This subtype is similar to the character string. The only difference is that you should use a character the database implementation has defined. Consequently, when you specify this subtype, the values you're dealing with should be compatible with the characters specified by your system. SQL users utilize a national character string to store data in different human languages (e.g. English, French, Italian, etc.) within a single database.

- Bit String – Here, you should base your permitted values on binary digits (i.e. data bits) instead of collations or character sets. That means this subtype can handle zeroes and ones only.

- Binary String – A binary string has many similarities with a bit string. The main difference is that the former uses bytes (not bits) in specifying the allowed values. Each byte is equivalent to eight bits, which is the main reason why SQL users refer to bytes as "octets."

The Datetime Type

You can use this data type to track times and dates. The SQL language supports three kinds of datetime data types:

- Date – This subtype specifies a date's day, month, and year value. The day value has two digits and goes from 01 to 31; the month value has two digits and goes from 01 to 12; and the year value has four digits and goes from 0001 to 9999.

- Time – You can use this subtype to specify a time's second, minute, and hour value. All of these values have two digits. The second value goes from 00 to 61.999 (taking the "leap seconds" into account); the minute value goes from 00 to 59; and the hour value goes from 00 to 23.

- Timestamp – This subtype combines the data of DATE and TIME. It uses six fractional digits for the value of TIME. To change the number of fractional digits, you just have to indicate the number you want to use as a parameter (e.g. TIMESTAMP(5).

Interval

This data type has a close relationship with the datatime type. Basically, you will use an interval data type to show the difference between different datetime values. The SQL language supports the following subtypes:

- Day-Time Intervals - With this subtype, you can specify the interval between these values: seconds, minutes, hours, or days.
- Year-Month Intervals – Use this subtype to specify the interval between months, years, or both.

The Boolean Type

Programmers consider Boolean values as easy and straightforward pieces of information. The Boolean type uses a true/false format that accepts three values only: unknown, false, and true. Null values evaluate to unknown. In this computer language, you'll use null values to express unknown or undefined values.

You may use Boolean values in your SQL expressions and queries to perform comparisons. Comparisons involving Boolean information follow this logic:

- A "true" has a higher value than a "false."
- You will get "unknown" if you will perform a comparison involving a null value.
- You can assign "unknown" to columns that support it.

To use this data type, you should type BOOLEAN without any parameter. Here's an example:

BOOK_HAS_SEQUEL BOOLEAN

The column named BOOK_HAS_SEQUEL will reject values that are not "unknown," "false," or "true."

The Numeric Type

As its name suggests, the numeric data type specifies numbers as allowed values. This type has a scale and a precision. The "scale" is the total number of integers found in the fractional part of a value. The "precision," on the other hand, is the number of integers that you can store. For instance, the scale and precision of 9.999 is 3 and 4, respectively. Keep in mind that a value's scale should always be positive and lower than the precision. If the scale of your value is zero, you are dealing with a whole number (i.e. a number that doesn't have any fractional part).

The SQL language supports two subtypes of the numeric data type. These subtypes are:

- Exact Numeric – When using this subtype, your permitted values must have a scale and a precision.
- Approximate Numeric – This subtype doesn't accept scales. Thus, your allowed values may have a "floating" decimal point. Floating-point values are numbers that have a decimal point, but the placement of that decimal point is

not important. This is the reason why an approximate numeric data type "doesn't take a scale."

How to Use the Data Types of SQL

In this part of the book, you'll learn how to set the data type of new columns. Here, you will still use the CREATE TABLE command. Analyze the following example:

CREATE TABLE AUTHORS

(AUTHOR_ID   INT ,

 AUTHOR_NAME   CHARACTER(50) ,

 AUTHOR_DOB   DATE ,

 BOOK_IN_STOCK   BOOLEAN) ;

The column named AUTHOR_ID will take values that belong to the numeric type; the one named AUTHOR_NAME takes string values; the AUTHOR_DOB column accepts datetime values; and the BOOK_IN_STOCK column takes Boolean data only.

How to Specify the Default Value of a Column

One of the most powerful features of SQL is that it allows you to set the default value of a new column. You should use this feature while creating a table (i.e. while issuing CREATE TABLE). Here is the syntax that you should use while setting a column's default value:

(name of column) (type of data) DEFAULT (the default value)

The (type of data) and (name of column) parts, which you've encountered earlier, come before the SQL keyword DEFAULT. After that keyword, you need to specify the value you want to set as default. When setting a default value, you may use a literal (i.e. a data value of SQL), a user function (i.e. one that gives user-related data), or a datetime function.

Regardless of the value you set for (the default value), you should meet the requirements of your chosen data type. For instance, if you set a column so that it accepts numeric values only, you can't set "unknown" as its default value.

In the example found below, you'll use CREATE TABLE to generate a table called AUTHORS.

CREATE TABLE AUTHORS

(AUTHOR_ID   INT ,

  AUTHOR_NAME   CHARACTER(50) ,

  PLACE_OF_BIRTH -   CHARACTER(50   DEFAULT ' NULL '
) ;

As you can see, the column called PLACE_OF_BIRTH has 'NULL' as its default value. This value works since it meets the requirements of your chosen data type (i.e. CHARACTER). In addition, a pair of single quotation marks enclose the value involved.

Important Note: If you will insert a new entry and you don't want to populate the PLACE_OF_BIRTH column, the system will enter NULL on your behalf.

How to Alter an SQL Table

This part of the book will teach you a new command, which is ALTER TABLE. You can use this command to alter the base tables inside a database. The basic syntax of this command is:

ALTER TABLE (name of table)

  ADD {COLUMN} (definition of column)

| ALTER {COLUMN} (name of column)

     [DROP DEFAULT | SET DEFAULT (the default value)]

| DROP {COLUMN} (name of column) [RESTRICT | CASCADE]

This syntax lets you perform one of these actions: inserting a column, altering a column, or dropping a column.

Important Note: You can also use this command to remove or insert table constraints. Basically, table constraints are rules that limit what information you can enter into a table. They are part of a table's definition. However, they don't belong to specific definitions of columns.

The (definition of column) part of the second line has some similarities with the one used in CREATE TABLE. You need to set the column's name and domain/data type. Additionally, you may add a collation, constraint, or default clause. For instance, you may use the code below to insert another column (i.e. AUTHOR_DOB) to the table called AUTHORS:

ALTER TABLE AUTHORS

ADD COLUMN AUTHOR_DOB DATE;

The third line offers two possible actions: removing the default value or setting a new one. As an example, let's assume that the AUTHOR_DOB column has no default value. You may use the following code to assign a default for that column:

ALTER TABLE AUTHORS

ALTER COLUMN AUTHOR_DB SET DEFAULT ' N/A ' ;

To remove the default value, use this command:

37

ALTER TABLE AUTHORS

   ALTER COLUMN AUTHOR_DOB DROP DEFAULT ;

The last line of the syntax offers two choices for removing columns (and the data they contain). These options are: RESTRICT and CASCADE. The former will delete a column if there's no routine, view, trigger, or constraint that points to it. The latter, on the other hand, deletes a column and its contents even if objects reference it. For instance, the following command removes AUTHOR_DOB and its data regardless of the current object dependencies:

ALTER TABLE AUTHORS

   DROP COLUMN AUTHOR_DOB CASCADE ;

ALTER TABLE is a useful command since table definitions often change. However, just like other SQL statements, this command may have different features based on the database implementation you are using. For instance, RESTRICT and CASCADE are not available in SQL Server. Meanwhile, Oracle requires you to type CASCADE CONSTRAINTS instead of CASCADE (this implementation doesn't support RESTRICT explicitly).

How to Delete an SQL Table

In SQL, deleting tables and their contents is easy and simple. Here is the syntax that you need to use:

DROP TABLE (name of table) [RESTRICT | CASCADE]

When using this command, you have to choose either RESTRICT or CASCADE. The RESTRICT option deletes the table if no other objects "depend" on it. CASCADE, however, removes the table and all of the objects that point to it. For instance, the command given below removes the table named AUTHORS and all of its contents, even if objects currently point to it:

DROP TABLE AUTHORS CASCADE ;

Chapter 4: How to Ensure Data Integrity

SQL databases don't just store information. They need to make sure that the information they store is reliable. If the information's integrity has been compromised, its reliability becomes questionable. If the data is unreliable, the database that contains it also becomes unreliable.

To secure data integrity, SQL offers a wide range of rules that can limit the values a table can hold. These rules, known as "integrity constraints," work on columns and tables. This chapter will explain each kind of constraint. It will also teach you how to apply the said constraints to your own database.

Integrity Constraints – The Basics

SQL users divide integrity constraints into the following categories:

- The Assertions – You need to define this constraint inside a separate definition (which is called the "assertion definition"). That means you won't indicate an assertion in your table's definition. In SQL, you may apply an assertion to multiple tables.

- The Table-Related Constraints – This is a constraint that you need to define inside a table's definition. You may define a constraint as a component of a table's or column's definition.

- The Domain Constraints – Similar to the assertions, you need to create domain constraints in a separate definition. This kind of constraint works on the column/s that you declared inside the domain involved.

Table-related constraints offer various constraint options. Consequently, it is the most popular category of integrity constraints these days. You can divide this category into two: column constraints and table constraints. The former belong to the definition of a column. The latter, on the other hand, act as elements of a table.

The table and column constraints work with different kinds of constraints. The domain constraints and assertions, however, can work with one constraint type only.

The Not Null Constraint

In the previous chapter, you learned that "null" represents an unknown/undefined value. Keep in mind that undefined/unknown is different from zeroes, blanks, default values, and empty strings. Rather, it signifies the absence of a value. You may consider this value as a "flag" (i.e. a bit, number, or character that expresses some data regarding a column). For null, if you leave a column empty, the system will place the "flag" to indicate that there's an unknown value.

Columns have an attribute called "nullability." This attribute shows whether the columns can take unknown values or not. In SQL, columns are set to take null values. However, you may change this attribute according to your needs. To disable the nullability of a column, you just have to use the NOT NULL constraint. This constraint informs SQL that the column won't accept any null value.

In this language, you need to use NOT NULL on a column. That means you can't use this constraint on an assertion, domain constraint, or table-based constraint. Using NOT NULL is a simple process. You just have to add the syntax given below to your column definition:

(name of column) [(domain) | (data type)] NOT NULL

As an example, let's assume that you need to generate a table called FICTION_NOVEL_AUTHORS. This table needs three columns: AUTHOR_ID, AUTHOR_NAME, and AUTHOR_DOB. You need to ensure that each entry you'll add has values for AUTHOR_ID and AUTHOR_NAME. To accomplish this, you must insert the NOT NULL constraint into the definition of both columns. Here's the code:

CREATE TABLE FICTION_NOVEL_AUTHORS

(AUTHOR_ID   INT   NOT NULL ,

  AUTHOR_NAME   CHARACTER(50)   NOT NULL ,

  AUTHOR_DOB   CHARACTER(50)) ;

As you can see, this code didn't set NOT NULL for the AUTHOR_DOB column. Consequently, if a new entry doesn't have any value for AUTHOR_DOB, the system will insert a null value to that column.

The Unique Constraint

Table and column constraints accept unique constraints. In SQL, unique constraints belong to one of these types:

1. UNIQUE
2. PRIMARY KEY

Important Note: This part of the book will concentrate on the first type. You'll learn about the second one later.

Basically, you can use UNIQUE to make sure that a column won't accept duplicate values. This constraint will stop you from entering a value that already exists in the column.

Let's assume that you want to apply this constraint on the AUTHOR_DOB column. This way, you can make sure that the values inside that column are all unique. Now, let's say you realized that requiring dates of birth to be unique is a bad idea since people may be born on the same date. You may adjust your approach by placing the UNIQUE constraint on AUTHOR_NAME and AUTHOR_DOB. Here, the table will stop you from repeating an AUTHOR_NAME/AUTHOR_DOB pair. You may repeat values in the AUTHOR_NAME and AUTHOR_DOB columns. However, you can't reenter an exact pair that already exists in the table.

It is time for you to create your own UNIQUE constraints. Keep in mind that you may tag UNIQUE constraints as table constraints or column constraints. To generate column constraints, add them to the definition of a column. Here is the syntax:

(name of column) [(domain) | (data type)] UNIQUE

If you need to use the UNIQUE constraint on a table, you must insert it into the table definition as an element. The following syntax will show you how:

{ CONSTRAINT (name of constraint) }

UNIQUE < (name of column) { [, (name of column)] ... } >

As the syntax above shows, using UNIQUE on a table is more complicated than using the constraint on a column. However, you cannot apply UNIQUE on multiple columns. Regardless of how you use this constraint (i.e. either as a table constraint or a column constraint), you may define any number of UNIQUE constraints within each table definition.

Let's apply this constraint on a columnar level:

CREATE TABLE BOOK_LIBRARY

(AUTHOR_NAME   CHARACTER (50) ,

  BOOK_TITLE   CHARACTER (70) UNIQUE,

  PUBLISHED_DATE   INT) ;

You may also use UNIQUE on other columns. However, its result would be different from that of using a table constraint on multiple columns. The following code will illustrate this idea:

CREATE TABLE BOOK_LIBRARY

(AUTHOR_NAME   CHARACTER (50),

  BOOK_TITLE   CHARACTER (70),

  PUBLISHED_DATE   INT,

  CONSTRAINT UN_AUTHOR_BOOK UNIQUE (AUTHOR_NAME, BOOK_TITLE)) ;

Now, the AUTHOR_NAME and BOOK_TITLE columns must have unique values for the table to accept a new entry.

As you've read earlier, the UNIQUE constraint makes sure that one or more columns won't take duplicate values. That is an important rule to remember. However, you should also know that UNIQUE doesn't work on "null." Thus, a column will accept any number of null values even if you have set a UNIQUE constraint on it.

If you want to set your columns so that they will not accept a null value, you must use NOT NULL. Let's apply NOT NULL on the column definition of BOOK_TITLE:

CREATE TABLE BOOK_LIBRARY

(AUTHOR_NAME   CHARACTER (50),

  BOOK_TITLE   CHARACTER (70)   UNIQUE   NOT NULL,

  PUBLISHED_DATE   INT) ;

45

In SQL, you may also insert NOT NULL into column definitions that a table-level constraint is pointing to:

CREATE TABLE BOOK_LIBRARY

(AUTHOR_NAME   CHARACTER (50) ,

  BOOK_TITLE   CHARACTER (70) NOT NULL,

  PUBLISHED_DATE   INT,

  CONSTRAINT UN_AUTHOR_BOOK UNIQUE (BOOK_TITLE)
) ;

In both cases, the BOOK_TITLE column gets the constraint. That means BOOK_TITLE won't accept null or duplicate values.

The PRIMARY KEY Constraint

The PRIMARY KEY constraint is almost identical to the UNIQUE constraint. You may use a PRIMARY KEY to prevent duplicate entries. In addition, you may apply it to multiple columns and use it as a table constraint or a column constraint. The only difference is that PRIMARY KEY has two distinct restrictions. These restrictions are:

- If you will apply PRIMARY key on a column, that column won't accept any null value. Basically, you won't have to use the NOT NULL constraint on a column that has PRIMARY KEY.
- A table can't have multiple PRIMARY KEY constraints.

These restrictions exist because primary keys (also known as "unique identifiers") play an important role in each table. As discussed in the first chapter, tables cannot have duplicate rows. This rule is crucial since the SQL language cannot identify redundant rows. If you will change a row, all of its duplicates will also be affected.

You need to choose a primary key from the candidate keys of your database. Basically, candidate keys are groups of columns that identify rows in a unique manner. You may enforce a candidate key's uniqueness using UNIQUE or PRIMARY KEY. However, you must place one primary key on each table even if you didn't define any unique constraint. This requirement ensures the uniqueness of each data row.

To define a primary key, you need to indicate the column/s you want to use. You can complete this task through PRIMARY KEY (i.e. the SQL keyword). This process is similar to the one discussed in the previous section. When applying PRIMARY KEY on a new column, you should use this syntax:

(name of column) [(domain) | (data type)] PRIMARY KEY

To use PRIMARY key on a table, you must enter it as an element of the table you're working on. Check the syntax below:

{ CONSTRAINT (name of constraint) }

PRIMARY KEY < (name of column) {, (name of column)] ... } >

47

SQL allows you to define primary keys using column constraints. However, you can only use this feature on a single column. Analyze the following example:

CREATE TABLE FICTION_NOVEL_AUTHORS

(AUTHOR_ID   INT,

 AUTHOR_NAME   CHARACTER (50)   PRIMARY KEY ,

 PUBLISHER_ID   INT) ;

If you want to apply PRIMARY KEY on multiple columns (or store it as another definition), you may use it on the tabular level:

CREATE TABLE FICTION_NOVEL_AUTHORS

(AUTHOR_ID   INT,

 AUTHOR_NAME   CHARACTER (50) ,

 PUBLISHER_ID   INT,

 CONSTRAINT   PK_AUTHOR_ID PRIMARY KEY (AUTHOR_ID , AUTHOR_NAME)) ;

This approach places a primary key on two columns (i.e. AUTHOR_ID and AUTHOR_NAME). That means the paired values of the two columns need to be unique. However, duplicate values may exist inside any of the columns. Experienced database users refer to this kind of primary key as a "superkey." The term "superkey" means the primary key exceeds the number of required columns.

In most cases, you need to set both UNIQUE and PRIMARY KEY constraints on a table. To achieve this, you just have to define the involved constraints as normal. For instance, the code given below applies both of these constraints:

CREATE TABLE FICTION_NOVEL_AUTHORS

(AUTHOR_ID   INT,

  AUTHOR_NAME   CHARACTER (50) PRIMARY KEY ,

  PUBLISHER_ID   INT,

  CONSTRAINT UN_AUTHOR_NAME UNIQUE (AUTHOR_NAME)) ;

The following code will give you the same result:

CREATE TABLE FICTION_NOVEL_AUTHORS

(AUTHOR_ID   INT,

  AUTHOR_NAME   CHARACTER (50) -> UNIQUE,

  PUBLISHER_ID   INT,

  CONSTRAINT PK_PUBLISHER_ID PRIMARY KEY (PUBLISHER_ID)) ;

The FOREIGN KEY Constraints

The constraints discussed so far focus on securing the data integrity of a table. NOT NULL stops columns from taking null values. PRIMARY KEY and UNIQUE, on the other hand, guarantee that the values of one or more columns are unique. In this regard, FOREIGN KEY (i.e. another SQL constraint) is different. FOREIGN KEY, also called "referential constraint," focuses on how information inside a table works with the information within another table.

In the first chapter of this book, you learned that the tables of relational databases are interconnected. This connection ensures information integrity throughout the database. In addition, the connection between different tables results to "referential integrity." This kind of integrity makes sure that data manipulation done on one table won't affect the data inside other tables. The tables given below will help you understand this topic. Each of these tables, named PRODUCT_NAMES and PRODUCT_MANUFACTURERS, have one primary key:

PRODUCT_NAMES

PRODUCT_NAME_ID: INT	PRODUCT_NAME: CHARACTER (50)	MANUFACTURER_ID: INT
1001	X Pen	91
1002	Y Eraser	92
1003	Z Notebook	93

PRODUCT_MANUFACTURERS

MANUFACTURER_ID: INT	BUSINESS_NAME: CHARACTER (50)
91	THE PEN MAKERS INC.
92	THE ERASER MAKERS INC.
93	THE NOTEBOOK MAKERS INC.

The PRODUCT_NAME_ID column of the PRODUCT_NAMES table has a PRIMARY KEY. The MANUFACTURER_ID of the PRODUCT_MANUFACTURERS table has the same constraint. These columns are in yellow (see the tables above).

As you can see, the PRODUCT_NAMES table has a column called MANUFACTURER_ID. That column has the values of a column in the PRODUCT_MANUFACTURERS table. Actually, the MANUFACTURER_ID column of the PRODUCT_NAMES table can only accept values that come from the MANUFACTURER_ID column of the PRODUCT_MANUFACTURERS table.

Additionally, the changes that you'll make on the PRODUCT_NAMES table may affect the data stored in the PRODUCT_MANUFACTURERS table. If you will remove a manufacturer, you also need to remove the entry from the MANUFACTURER_ID column of the PRODUCT_NAMES table.

You can achieve this result using FOREIGN KEY. This constraint ensures the referential integrity of your database by preventing actions on any table from affecting the protected information.

Important Note: If a table has a foreign key, it is called "referencing table." The table a foreign key points to is called "referenced table."

While creating this kind of constraint, you need to obey the following guidelines:

- You must define a referenced column by using PRIMARY KEY or UNIQUE. Most SQL programmers choose PRIMARY KEY for this purpose.

- You may tag FOREIGN KEY constraints as column constraints or table constraints. You may work with any number of columns if you are using FOREIGN KEY as a table constraint. On the other hand, if you will use this constraint at the column-level, you can work on a single column only.

- A referencing table's foreign key should cover all of the columns you are trying to reference. In addition, the columns of the referencing table should match the data type of their counterparts (i.e. the columns being referenced). However, you don't have to use the same names for your referencing and referenced columns.

- You don't need to indicate reference columns manually. SQL will consider the columns of the referenced table's primary key as the referenced columns if you won't specify any column for the constraint. This process happens automatically.

You'll understand these guidelines once you have analyzed the examples given below. For now, let's analyze the syntax of this constraint. Here's the format that you must use to apply FOREIGN KEY at the columnar level:

(name of column) [(domain) | (data type)] { NOT NULL }

REFERENCES (name of the referenced table) { < (the referenced columns) > }

{ MATCH [SIMPLE | FULL | PARTIAL] }

{ (the referential action) }

To use this FOREIGN KEY as a tabular constraint, you need to insert it as a table's element. Here's the syntax:

{ CONSTRAINT (name of constraint) }

FOREIGN KEY < (the referencing column) { [, (the referencing column)] ... } >

REFERENCES (the referenced table) { < (the referenced column/s) > }

{ MATCH [SIMPLE | FULL | PARTIAL] }

{ (the referential action) }

You've probably noticed that FOREIGN KEY is more complex than the constraints you've seen so far. This complexity results from the constraint's option-filled syntax. However, generating this kind of constraint is easy and simple. Let's analyze a basic

53

example first:

```
CREATE TABLE PRODUCT_NAMES
( PRODUCT_NAME_ID -> INT,
  PRODUCT_NAME -> CHARACTER (50) ,
  MANUFACTURER_ID -> INT -> REFERENCES PRODUCT_MANUFACTURERS ) ;
```

This code applies the constraint on the column named MANUFACTURER_ID. To apply this constraint on a table, you just have to type REFERENCES and indicate the referenced table's name. In addition, the columns of this foreign key is equal to that of the referenced table's primary key. If you don't want to reference your target's primary key, you need to specify the column/s you want to use. For instance, REFERENCES PRODUCT_MANUFACTURERS (MANUFACTURER_ID).

Important Note: The FOREIGN KEY constraint requires an existing referenced table. In addition, that table must have a PRIMARY KEY or UNIQUE constraint.

For the second example, you will use FOREIGN KEY as a tabular constraint. The code you'll see below specifies the referenced column's name even if that information is not needed.

```
CREATE TABLE PRODUCT_NAMES
( PRODUCT_NAME_ID   INT,
    PRODUCT_NAME   CHARACTER (50) ,
```

MANUFACTURER_ID   INT,

CONSTRAINT TS_MANUFACTURER_ID FOREIGN KEY (MANUFACTURER_ID)

REFERENCES PRODUCT_MANUFACTURERS (MANUFACTURER_ID)) ;

You may consider the two lines at the bottom as the constraint's definition. The constraint's name, TS_MANUFACTURER_ID, comes after the keyword CONSTRAINT. You don't need to specify a name for your constraints since SQL will generate one for you in case this information is missing. On the other hand, you may want to set the name of your constraint manually since that value appears in errors (i.e. when SQL commands violate an existing constraint). In addition, the names you will provide are more recognizable than system-generated ones.

Next, you should set the kind of constraint you want to use. Then, enter the name of your referencing column (MANUFACTURER_ID for the current example). You will then place the constraint on that column. If you are dealing with multiple columns, you must separate the names using commas. Afterward, type REFERENCES as well as the referenced table's name. Lastly, enter the name of your referenced column.

That's it. Once you have defined this constraint, the MANUFACTURER_ID column of PRODUCT_NAMES won't take values except those that are already listed in the PRODUCT_MANUFACTURERS table's primary key. As you can see, a foreign key doesn't need to hold unique values. You may repeat the values inside your foreign keys as many times as you want, unless you placed the UNIQUE constraint on the column you're working on.

Now, let's apply this constraint on multiple columns. You should master this technique before studying the remaining elements of the constraint's syntax. For this example, let's use two tables: BOOK_AUTHORS and BOOK_GENRES.

The table named BOOK_AUTHORS has a primary key defined in the AUTHOR_NAME and AUTHOR_DOB columns. The SQL statement found below generates a table called BOOK_GENRES. This table has a foreign key consisting of the AUTHOR_DOB and DATE_OF_BIRTH columns.

CREATE TABLE BOOK_GENRES

(AUTHOR_NAME   CHARACTER (50),

DATE_OF_BIRTH   DATE,

GENRE_ID   INT,

CONSTRAINT TS_BOOK_AUTHORS FOREIGN KEY (AUTHOR_NAME, DATE_OF_BIRTH) REFERENCES BOOK_AUTHORS (AUTHOR_NAME, AUTHOR_DOB)) ;

This code has a pair of referenced columns (i.e. AUTHOR_NAME, AUTHOR_DOB) and a pair of referencing columns (i.e. AUTHOR_NAME and DATE_OF_BIRTH). The columns named AUTHOR_NAME inside the data tables contain the same type of data. The data type of the DATE_OF_BIRTH column is the same as that of AUTHOR_DOB. As this example shows, the name of a referenced column doesn't need to match that of its referencing counterpart.

The MATCH Part

Now, let's discuss another part of the constraint's syntax:

{ MATCH [SIMPLE | FULL | PARTIAL] }

The curly braces show that this clause is optional. The main function of this clause is to let you choose how to handle null values inside a foreign key column, considering the values that you may add to a referencing column. This clause won't work on columns that don't accept null values.

This part of the syntax offers three choices:

- SIMPLE – If you will choose this option, and at least one of your referencing columns has a null value, you may place any value on the rest of the referencing columns. The system will automatically trigger this option if you won't specify the MATCH section of your FOREIGN KEY's definition.
- FULL – This option requires all of your referencing columns to accept null values; otherwise, none of them can accept a null value.
- PARTIAL – With this option, you may place null values on your referencing columns if other referencing columns contain values that match their respective referenced columns.

The (referential action) Part

This is the final section of the FOREIGN KEY syntax. Just like the MATCH part, "referential action" is completely optional. You can use this clause to specify which actions to take while updating or removing information from one or more referenced columns.

For instance, let's assume that you want to remove an entry from the primary key of a table. If a foreign key references the primary key you're working on, your desired action will violate the constraint. You should always include the data of your referencing columns inside your referenced columns.

When using this clause, you will set a specific action to the referencing table's definition. This action will occur once your referenced table gets changed. Here is the syntax that you must use:

ON UPDATE (the referential action) { ON DELETE (the referential action) } | ON DELETE (the referential action) { ON UPDATE (the referential action) } (the referential action) ::=

RESTRICT | SET NULL | CASCADE | NO ACTION | SET DEFAULT

According to this syntax, you may set ON DELETE, ON UPDATE, or both. These clauses can accept one of the following actions:

- RESTRICT – This referential action prevents you from performing updates or deletions that can violate the FOREIGN KEY constraint. The information inside a referencing column cannot violate FOREIGN KEY.

- SET NULL – This action changes the values of a referencing column to "null" if its corresponding referenced column gets removed or updated. If you want to use this option, make sure that your referencing columns accept null values.

- CASCADE – With this referential action, the changes you'll apply on a referenced column will also be applied to its referencing column.

- NO ACTION – Just like RESTRICT, NO ACTION stops you from performing actions that will violate FOREIGN KEY. The main difference is that NO ACTION allows data violations while you are executing an SQL command. However, the information within your foreign key will not be violated once the command has been executed.

- SET DEFAULT – With this option, you may set a referencing column to its default value by updating or deleting the data inside the corresponding referenced column. This referential action won't work if your referencing columns don't have default values.

To use this clause, you just have to insert it to the last part of a FOREIGN KEY's definition. Here's an example:

CREATE TABLE AUTHORS_ GENRES

(AUTHOR_NAME   CHARACTER (50) ,

DATE_OF_BIRTH   DATE,

GENRE_ID   INT,

CONSTRAINT TS_BOOK_AUTHORS FOREIGN KEY (AUTHOR_NAME, DATE_ OF_BIRTH) REFERENCES BOOK_AUTHORS ON DELETE RESTRICT ON UPDATE

RESTRICT) ;

The CHECK Constraint

You can apply this constraint on a table, column, domain, or inside an assertion. This constraint lets you set which values to place inside your columns. You may use different conditions (e.g. value ranges) that define which values your columns may hold.

According to SQL programmers, the CHECK constraint is the most complex and flexible constraint currently available. However, this constraint has a simple syntax. To use CHECK as a column constraint, add the syntax below to your column definition:

(name of column) [(domain) | (data type)] CHECK < (the search condition) >

If you want to use this constraint on a table, insert the syntax below to your table's definition:

{ CONSTRAINT (name of constraint) } CHECK < (the search condition) >

Important Note: You'll know how to use this constraint on assertions and domains later.

As this syntax shows, CHECK is easy to understand. However, its search condition may involve complex and extensive values. This constraint tests the assigned search condition for the SQL commands that try to alter the information inside a column protected by CHECK. If the result of the test is TRUE, the commands will run; if the result is false, the system will cancel the commands and display some error messages.

You need to analyze examples in order to master this clause. However, almost all components of the search condition involve predicates. Predicates are expressions that work on values. In SQL, you may use a predicate to compare different values (e.g. COLUMN_3 < 5). The "less than" predicate checks whether the values inside COLUMN_3 are less than 5.

Most components of the search condition also utilize subqueries. Basically, subqueries are expressions that act as components of other expressions. You will use a subquery if an expression needs to access or compute different layers of information. For instance, an expression might need to access TABLE_X to insert information to TABLE_Z.

For now, let's focus on the basics of the CHECK constraint. In the example below, CHECK defines the highest and lowest values that you may enter in a column. This table definition generates a CHECK constraint and three columns:

CREATE TABLE BOOK_TITLES

(BOOK_ID   INT,

  BOOK_TITLE   CHARACTER (50) NOT NULL,

  STOCK_AVAILABILITY   INT,

  CONSTRAINT TS_STOCK_AVAILABILITY (

STOCK_AVAILABILITY < 50 AND STOCK_AVAILABILITY > 1)
) ;

The resulting table will reject values that are outside the 1-50 range. Here's another way of writing the table:

CREATE TABLE BOOK_TITLES

(BOOK_ID   INT,

  BOOK_TITLE   CHARACTER (50) NOT NULL,

  STOCK_AVAILABILITY INT CHECK (STOCK_AVAILABILITY < 50 AND STOCK AVAILABILITY > 1)) ;

Now, let's analyze the condition clause of these statements. This clause tells SQL that all of the values added to the STOCK_AVAILABILITY column should be lower than 50. The keyword AND informs SQL that there's another condition that must be applied. Lastly, the clause tells SQL that each value added to the said column should be higher than 1. To put it simply, each value should be lower than 50 and higher than 1.

This constraint also allows you to just list your "acceptable values." SQL users consider this as a powerful option when it comes to values that won't be changed regularly. In the next example, you will use the CHECK constraint to define a book's genre:

CREATE TABLE BOOK_TITLES

(BOOK_ID   INT,

BOOK_TITLE   CHARACTER (50),

GENRE   CHAR (10),

CONSTRAINT TS_GENRE CHECK (GENRE IN (' DRAMA ' , ' HORROR ' , ' SELF HELP ' , ' ACTION ' , ' MYSTERY ' , ' ROMANCE '))) ;

Each value inside the GENRE column should be included in the listed genres of the condition. The system will give you an error message if you will enter values other than "null" or the six listed genres. As you can see, this statement uses IN (i.e. an SQL operator). Basically, IN makes sure that the values within GENRE are included in the listed entries.

This constraint can be extremely confusing since it involves a lot of parentheses. You may simplify your SQL codes by dividing them into multiple lines. As an example, let's rewrite the code given above:

CREATE TABLE BOOK_TITLES

(

BOOK_ID   INT,

BOOK_TITLE   CHAR (50),

GENRE   CHAR (10),

CONSTRAINT TS_GENRE CHECK

(

GENRE IN

         ('DRAMA ' , ' HORROR ' , ' SELF HELP ' , ' ACTION ' , ' MYSTERY ' , ' ROMANCE '

)

)

);

This style of writing SQL commands ensures code readability. Here, you need to indent the parentheses and their contents so that they show their position clearly in the different layers of the SQL statement. By using this style, you can quickly identify the clauses placed in each pair of parentheses. Additionally, this statement works like the previous one. The only drawback of this style is that you need to use lots of space.

Let's analyze another example:

CREATE TABLE BOOK_TITLES

(BOOK_ID   INT,

  BOOK_TITLE   CHAR (50) ,

  STOCK_AVAILABILITY   INT,

  CONSTRAINT TS_STOCK_AVAILABILITY CHECK ((STOCK_AVAILABILITY BETWEEN 1 AND 50) OR (STOCK_AVAILABILITY BETWEEN 79 AND 90))) ;

This code uses BETWEEN (i.e. another SQL operator) to set a range that includes the lowest and highest points. Because it has two ranges, it separates the range specifications using parentheses. The OR keyword connects the range specifications.

Basically, OR tells SQL that one of the conditions need to be satisfied. Consequently, the values you will enter in the column named STOCK_AVAILABILITY should be from 1 through 50 or from 79 through 90.

How to Define an Assertion

Assertions are CHECK constraints that you can apply on multiple tables. Because of this, you can't create assertions while defining a table. Here's the syntax that you must use while creating an assertion:

CREATE ASSERTION (name of constraint) CHECK (the search conditions)

Defining an assertion is similar to defining a table-level CHECK constraint. After typing CHECK, you need to specify the search condition/s.

Let's analyze a new example. Assume that the BOOK_TITLES table has a column that holds the quantity of books in stock. The total for this table should always be lower than your desired inventory. This example uses an assertion to check whether or not the total of the STOCK_AVAILABILITY column is lower than 3000.

CREATE ASSERTION LIMIT_STOCK_AVAILABILITY CHECK ((SELECT SUM (STOCK_AVAILABILITY) FROM BOOK_TITLES) < 3000) ;

This statement uses a subquery (i.e. "SELECT SUM (STOCK_AVAILABILITY) FROM BOOK_TITLES") and compares it with 3000. The subquery starts with an SQL keyword, SELECT, which queries information from any table. The SQL function called SUM adds up all of the values inside STOCK_AVAILABILITY. The keyword FROM, on the other hand, sets the column that holds the table. The system will then compare the subquery's result to 3000. You will get an error message if you'll add an entry to the STOCK_AVAILABILITY column that makes the total exceed 3000.

How to Create a Domain and a Domain Constraint

As mentioned earlier, you may also insert the CHECK constraint into your domain definitions. This kind of constraint is similar to the ones you've seen earlier. The only difference is that you won't attach a domain constraint to a particular table or column. Actually, a domain constraint uses VALUE, another SQL keyword, while referring to a value inside a column specified for that domain. Now, let's discuss the syntax you need to use while generating new domains:

CREATE DOMAIN (name of domain) {AS} (type of data)

{ DEFAULT (the default value) }

{ CONSTRAINT (name of constraint) } CHECK < (the search condition) >

This syntax has elements you've seen before. You've learned about default clauses and data types in the third chapter. The definition of the constraint, on the other hand, has some similarities with the ones discussed in the last few sections.

For the example below, you will generate an INT-type domain. This domain can only accept values between 1 and 50:

CREATE DOMAIN BOOK_QUANTITY AS INT CONSTRAINT TS_BOOK_QUANTITY CHECK (VALUE BETWEEN 1 and 50) ;

This example involves one new item, which is the VALUE keyword. As mentioned earlier, this keyword refers to a column's value specified using the BOOK_QUANTITY domain. Consequently, you will get an error message if you will enter a value that doesn't satisfy the assigned condition (i.e. each value must be between 1 and 50).

Chapter 5: How to Create an SQL View

Your database stores SQL information using "persistent" (i.e. permanent) tables. However, persistent tables can be impractical if you just want to check particular entries from one or more tables. Because of this, the SQL language allows you to use "views" (also called "viewed tables").

Views are virtual tables whose definitions act as schema objects. The main difference between views and persistent tables is that the former doesn't store any data. Actually, viewed tables don't really exist – only their definition exists. This definition lets you choose specific data from a table or a group of tables, according to the definition's query statements. To invoke a view, you just have to include its name in your query as if its an ordinary table.

How to Add a View to a Database

Views become extremely useful when you're trying to access various kinds of information. If you will use a view, you may define complicated queries and save them inside a view definition. Rather than typing queries each time you use them, you may just call the view. In addition, views allow you to present data to other people without showing any unnecessary or confidential information.

For instance, you might need to allow some users to access certain parts of employee records. However, you don't want the said users to access the SSN (i.e. social security number) or pay rates of the listed employees. Here, you may generate views that show only the data needed by the users.

How to Define an SQL View

In SQL, the most basic view that you can create is one which points to a single table and collects information from columns without changing anything. Here is the basic syntax of a view:

CREATE VIEW (name of view) { < (name of the view's columns) > }

AS (the query)

{ WITH CHECK OPTION }

Important Note: This part of the book will focus on the first and second lines of the format. You'll learn about the third line later.

You need to set the view's name in the first part of the definition. Additionally, you should name the view's columns if you are facing any of these circumstances:

- If you need to perform an operation to get the column's values, instead of just copying them from a table.
- If you are working with duplicate column names. This situation happens when you combine tables.

You may set names for your columns even if you don't need to. For instance, you may assign logical names to your columns so that even an inexperienced user can understand them.

The second part of the format has a mandatory keyword (i.e. AS) and a placeholder for the query. Despite its apparent simplicity, the query placeholder may involve a complicated structure of SQL statements that perform different operations.

Let's analyze a basic example:

CREATE VIEW BOOKS_IN_STOCK

(BOOK_TITLE, AUTHOR, STOCK_AVAILABILITY) AS

SELECT BOOK_TITLE, AUTHOR, STOCK_AVAILABILITY

FROM BOOK_INVENTORY

This sample is one of the simplest views that you can create. It gets three columns from a table. Remember that SQL isn't strict when it comes to line breaks and spaces. For instance, while creating a view, you may list the column names (if applicable) on a separate line. Database management systems won't care which coding technique you'll use. However, you can ensure the readability of your codes by adopting a coding style.

At this point, let's dissect the sample code given above. The first part sets BOOKS_IN_STOCK as the view's name. The second part sets the name of the columns and contains the SQL keyword AS.

If you won't specify the names you want to use, the view's columns will just copy the names of the table's columns. The last two lines hold the search expression, which is a SELECT statement. Here it is:

SELECT BOOK_TITLE, AUTHOR, STOCK_AVAILABILITY

FROM BOOK_INVENTORY

This is one of the most popular statements in the SQL language. SELECT is flexible and extensive: it allows you to write complex queries that give the exact kind of information you need.

The SELECT statement of this example is a basic one. It only has two clauses: SELECT and FROM. The first clause sets the column to be returned. The second clause, however, sets the table where the information will be pulled from. Once you call the BOOKS_IN_STOCKS view, you will actually call the embedded SELECT command of the view. This action gets the information from the correct table/s.

For the second example, you'll create a view that has an extra clause:

CREATE VIEW BOOKS_IN_STOCK_80s

(BOOK_TITLE, YEAR_PUBLISHED, STOCK_AVAILABILITY) AS

SELECT BOOK_TITLE, YEAR_PUBLISHED, STOCK_AVAILABILITY

FROM BOOK_INVENTORY

WHERE YEAR_PUBLISHED >1979 AND YEAR_PUBLISHED < 1990;

The last clause sets a criterion that should be satisfied for the system to retrieve data. This example is similar to the previous one. The only difference is that, rather than pulling the authors' information, it filters search results based on the year each book was published.

Important Note: The contents of the last clause don't affect the source table in any way. They work only on the information returned by the view.

You may use WHERE in your SELECT statements to set different types of criteria. For instance, you can use this clause to combine tables. Check the following code:

CREATE VIEW BOOK_PUBLISHERS

(BOOK_TITLE, PUBLISHER_NAME) AS

 SELECT BOOK_INVENTORY .BOOK_TITLE, TAGS .PUBLISHER_NAME

 FROM BOOK_INVENTORY, TAGS

 WHERE BOOK_INVENTORY .TAG_ID = TAGS .TAG_ID;

This code creates a view named BOOK_PUBLISHERS. The BOOK_PUBLISHERS view contains two columns: BOOK_TITLE and PUBLISHER_NAME. With this view, you'll get data from two different sources: (1) the BOOK_TITLE column of the BOOK_INVENTORY table and (2) the PUBLISHER_NAME column of the TABS table.

For now, let's focus on the third clause (i.e. the SELECT statement). This clause qualifies the columns based on the name of their respective tables (e.g. BOOK_INVENTORY .BOOK_TITLE). If you are joining tables, you need to qualify the names of each table to avoid confusion. Obviously, columns can be highly confusing if they have duplicate names. However, if you're dealing with simple column names, you may omit the name of your tables. For instance, your SELECT clause might look like this:

SELECT BOOK_TITLE, PUBLISHER_NAME

Now, let's discuss the statement's FROM section. While combining tables, you need to name all of the tables you want to use. Separate the entries using commas. Aside from the concern regarding duplicate names, this clause is identical to that of the previous examples.

WHERE, the last clause of this statement, matches data rows together. This clause is important since, if you won't use it, you won't be able to match values you've gathered from different tables. In the current example, the values inside the TAG_ID column of BOOK_INVENTORY should match the values inside the TAG_ID column of the table named TAGS.

SQL allows you to qualify a query by expanding the latter's WHERE clause. In the next example, WHERE restricts the returned rows to those that hold "999" in the BOOK_INVENTORY table's TAG_ID column:

CREATE VIEW BOOK_PUBLISHERS

(BOOK_TITLE, BOOK_PUBLISHER) AS

SELECT BOOK_INVENTORY .BOOK_TITLE, TAGS .BOOK_PUBLISHER

FROM BOOK_INVENTORY, TAGS

WHERE BOOK_INVENTORY .TAG_ID = TAGS .TAG_ID

AND BOOK_INVENTORY .TAG_ID = 999;

Let's work on another example. Similar to the examples you've seen earlier, this view collects information from a single table. This view, however, performs computations that return the modified information. Here is the statement:

CREATE VIEW BOOK_DISCOUNTS

(BOOK_TITLE, ORIGINAL_PRICE, REDUCED_PRICE) AS

SELECT BOOK_TITLE, ORIGINAL_PRICE, REDUCED_PRICE * 0.8

FROM BOOK_INVENTORY;

This statement creates a view that has three columns: BOOK_TITLE, ORIGINAL_PRICE, and REDUCED_PRICE. Here, SELECT indicates the columns that hold the needed information. The statement defines BOOK_TITLE and ORIGINAL_PRICE using the methods discussed in the previous examples. The system will copy the data inside the BOOK_INVENTORY table's BOOK_TITLE and ORIGINAL_PRICE columns. Then, the system will paste the data to the columns of the same name inside the BOOK_DISCOUNTS view.

The last column is different, however. Aside from taking values from its corresponding column, it multiplies the collected values by 0.8 (i.e. 80%). This way, the system will determine the correct values to display in the view's REDUCED_PRICE column.

SQL also allows you to insert the WHERE clause to your SELECT statements. Here's an example:

CREATE VIEW BOOK_DISCOUNTS

(BOOK_TITLE, ORIGINAL_PRICE, REDUCED_PRICE) AS

  SELECT BOOK_TITLE, ORIGINAL_PRICE, REDUCED PRICE * 0.8

  FROM BOOK_INVENTORY

  WHERE STOCK_AVAILABILITY > 20;

This WHERE clause limits the search to those entries whose STOCK_AVAILABILITY value is higher than 20. As this example shows, you may perform comparisons on columns that are included in the view.

How to Create an Updateable View

In the SQL language, some views allow you to perform updates. Simply put, you may use a view to alter the information (i.e. add new rows and/or alter existing information) inside the table you're working on. The "updateability" of a view depends on its SELECT statement. Usually, views that involve simple SELECT statements have higher chances of becoming updateable.

Remember that SQL doesn't have any syntax for creating updateable views. Rather, you need to write a SELECT statement that adheres to certain standards. This is the only way for you to create an updateable view.

The examples you've seen in this chapter imply that the SELECT statement serves as the search expression of a CREATE VIEW command. To be precise, query expressions may belong to different kinds of expressions. As an SQL user, you'll be dealing with query specifications most of the time. Query expressions are SQL expressions that start with SELECT and contains different elements. To retain the simplicity of this book, let's assume that SELECT is a query specification. Database products also use this assumption so it is certainly effective.

Here are the things you need to remember while writing an updateable view:

- You can't summarize, combine, or automatically delete the information inside the view.
- The table you're working with should have at least one updateable column.

- Every column inside the view should point to a single column in a table.

- Every row inside the view should point to a single row in a table.

How to Drop a View

In some cases, you need to delete a view from a database. To accomplish this task, you need to use the following syntax:

DROP VIEW (name of the view);

The system will delete the view as soon as you run this statement. However, the process won't affect the underlying information (i.e. the data stored inside the actual tables). After dropping a view, you may recreate it or use its name to generate another view. Let's analyze a basic example:

DROP VIEW BOOK_PUBLISHERS;

This command will delete the BOOK_PUBLISHERS view from the database. However, the underlying information will be unaffected.

Chapter 6: Database Security

Security is an important element of every database. You need to make sure that your database is safe from unauthorized users who may view or alter data. Meanwhile, you also need to ensure that authorized users can access and/or change data without any problems. The best solution for this problem is to provide each user with the privileges he/she needs to do his/her job.

To protect databases, SQL has a security scheme that lets you specify which database users can view specific information. This scheme also allows you to set what actions each user can perform. This security scheme (or model) relies on authorization identifiers. As you've learned in the second chapter, authorization identifiers are objects that represent one or more users that can access/modify the information inside the database.

This chapter will explain SQL's security model. It will also teach you how to use authorization identifiers. If you want to be an effective SQL user, you need to read this material carefully.

The Security Model of SQL

The security of your database relies on authorization identifiers. You can use these identifiers to allow other people to access and/or alter your database entries. If an authorization identifier lacks the right privileges to alter a certain object, the user won't be able to change the information inside that object. Additionally, you may configure each identifier with various kinds of privileges.

In SQL, an authorization identifier can be a user identifier (i.e. "user") or a role name (i.e. "role"). A "user" is a security profile that may represent a program, a person, or a service. SQL doesn't have specific rules regarding the creation of a user. You may tie the identifier to the OS (i.e. operating system) where the database system runs. Alternatively, you may create user identifiers inside the database system itself.

A role is a group of access rights that you may assign to users or other roles. If a certain role has access to an object, all users and roles you've assigned that role to can access the said object.

SQL users often utilize roles to provide uniform sets of access rights to other authorization identifiers. One of the main benefits offered by a role is that it can exist without any user identifier. That means you can create a role before creating a user. In addition, a role will stay n the database even if you have deleted all of your user identifiers. This functionality allows you to implement a flexible process for administering access rights.

The SQL language has a special authorization identifier called PUBLIC. This identifier covers all of the database users. Similar to other identifiers, you may assign access rights to a PUBLIC profile.

Important Note: You need to be careful when assigning access rights to the PUBLIC identifier. Users might utilize that identifier for unauthorized purposes.

Creating and Deleting a Role

Generating new roles is a simple process. The syntax has two clauses: an optional clause and a mandatory clause.

CREATE ROLE (name of role)

{ WITH ADMIN [CURRENT_ROLE | CURRENT_USER] }

As you can see, CREATE ROLE is the only mandatory section of this statement. You don't need to set the statement's WITH ADMIN part. Actually, SQL users rarely set that clause. WITH ADMIN becomes important only if your current role name/user identifier pair doesn't have any null value.

Let's use the syntax to create a role:

CREATE ROLE READERS;

That's it. After creating this role, you will be able to grant it to users or other roles.

To drop (or delete) a role, you just have to use the following syntax:

DROP ROLE (name of role)

This syntax has a single requirement: the name of the role you want to delete. The following example will show you how this syntax works:

DROP ROLE READERS;

Granting and Revoking a Privilege

Whenever you grant a privilege, you are actually linking a privilege to an authorization identifier. You will place this privilege/authorization identifier pair on an object, allowing the former to access the latter based on the defined privileges. Here is the syntax that you must use when granting privileges:

GRANT [(list of privileges) | ALL PRIVILEGES]

ON (type of object) (name of object)

TO [(list of authorization identifiers) | PUBLIC] { WITH GRANT OPTION }

{ GRANTED BY [CURRENT_ROLE | CURRENT_USER] }

This syntax has three mandatory clauses, namely: ON, TO and GRANT. The last two clauses, GRANTED BY and WITH GRANT OPTION, are completely optional.

The process of revoking privileges is simple and easy. You just have to use the syntax given below:

REVOKE { GRANT OPTION FOR } [(list of privileges) | ALL PRIVILEGES]

ON (type of object) name of object)

FROM [{ list of authorization identifiers) | PUBLIC }

Conclusion

This book discussed the most important ideas and principles related to SQL. By utilizing the tips, syntax, and coding styles presented in this material, you will be a skilled SQL programmer in no time.

The next step is to read more books about SQL programming and continue writing your own codes. Keep in mind that computer languages such as SQL are too complex to be mastered quickly. Thus, if you're planning to use SQL on a regular basis, you should get all of the SQL-related reading materials available to you. This style of collecting valuable information can help you master any computer language.

Additionally, you need to practice your skills regularly. Reading books is good. However, that is not enough to help you become a skilled SQL user. You also need to use the knowledge you've gained. By creating actual tables and databases, you'll gain the skills and experience required to become an expert.

I wish you the best of luck!

Robert Dwight

Printed in Great Britain
by Amazon